DYING AND LIVING FOR ALLAH

Dying and Living for Allah

THE LAST WILL OF
KHURRAM MURAD

Translated by
Syed Abu Ahmad Akif

THE ISLAMIC FOUNDATION

Published by

THE ISLAMIC FOUNDATION,

Markfield Conference Centre,
Ratby Lane, Markfield,
Leicester LE67 9SY, United Kingdom
Main Building - Tel: (01530) 244944/5, Fax: (01530) 244946
Publications - Tel: (01530) 249230, Fax: (01530) 249656
E-Mail: i.foundation@islamic-foundation.org.uk
Publication E-Mail: publications@islamic-foundation.com
Website: www.islamic-foundation.org.uk

QURAN HOUSE, P.O. Box 30611, Nairobi, Kenya

P.M.B. 3193, Kano, Nigeria

ISBN 13: 978 0 86037 336 0

Typeset by: N.A. Qaddoura
Cover design: Imtiaze A. Manjra
Printed in Great Britain by: Antony Rowe Ltd, Chippenham, Wiltshire

باسمه تعالى

Contents

Foreword

The Prophet Muḥammad ﷺ has beautifully summed up the essential message of Islam in two words *al-Dīn al-Naṣīḥah*,[1] that is Islam is nothing but 'good advice'. In fact, while *naṣīḥah* is good advice, it is more than mere advice – it is sincerity, loyalty, deep concern, purification of relationships, separating the grain from the chaff, wishing good, commanding right and discouraging evil, all rolled into one.

Naṣaḥat al-'Asal means purifying and distilling honey from the honeycomb. *Naṣaḥat al-Qalb* means cleansing of the heart from all impurities and unwholesome traits. *Naṣīḥah* as such has at least two dimensions: firstly, a deep sense of sincerity and well wishing based on purity of heart and loyalty to the truth; secondly, building all relationships on foundations of truth and justice, i.e. giving everyone their due, fulfilling all rights and obligations. *Naṣīḥah* covers the whole spectrum of existence, from faith in Allah ﷻ, through correct relationship with Allah ﷻ,

1. Muslim: as reported by Tamīm Al-Dārī.

His Prophet, peace be upon him, His Book, to building correct relationships and fulfilling all obligations in respect of the Muslim people and their leadership. This is exactly what has been so majestically encapsulated in the *Sūrah al-'Aṣr* in the Qur'ān.

> *Time is witness!*
> *Verily, Man is indeed in a state of loss,*
> *Except – those who attain faith and do good deeds, and enjoin upon one another the keeping of truth (Right) and be patient in adversity.*
>
> (Qur'ān 103:1-3)

Naṣīḥah, when made with greater intensity and force, almost bordering on command, becomes *waṣiyyah* – advising, commending and enjoining. While *naṣīḥah* and *waṣiyyah* is a life-long process, *waṣiyyah* more specifically is the last will and testament that a person makes, enjoining his kith and kin to fulfil his wishes after his death. Commanded by the Qur'ān and *Sunnah*, *Waṣiyyah* is not merely confined to one's financial matters. The tradition of the Prophets of Allah and other pious and God-fearing people is that along with financial matters, particularly dedicating a part (upto one-third) of one's wealth for good purposes, *naṣīḥah* is made to the near and dear ones to care for their *ākhirah*, to be loyal to their Lord, to fulfil their responsibilities towards others, to be particular in meeting obligations due to human beings (*ḥuqūq al-'ibād*) and to share the Divine message with all human beings, by commending and commanding what is good and forbidding what is wrong. Prophets Ibrāhīm and Ya'qūb are mentioned in the Qur'ān to have made this *waṣiyyah* to their children.

> *And Abraham enjoined the same upon his children and so did Jacob; 'My children! Behold, Allah has chosen this religion for you. Remain till death in submission to Him'.*
>
> *Nay, but you were witness O children of Israel, that when death was approaching Jacob, he said to his sons: 'Whom will you worship (serve) after me?' They answered: 'We shall serve your God, the God of your forefathers, Abraham, Ismael and Isaac: the one God and unto Him do we submit'.*[2]

So was the *waṣiyyah* of Luqmān, the wise:

> *And he, [Luqmān] spoke with his son, enjoining him: 'O my dear son! Do not ascribe divine power to anyone besides God – for behold, such (a false) ascribing of divinity is indeed an awesome wrong!'*
>
> *And (God says) We have enjoined upon man goodness towards his parents: his mother bore him by bearing strain upon strain, and his utter dependence on her lasted two years. Be grateful towards Me and towards your parents. To Me is your final Goal.*
>
> *[Revere your parents;] yet should they endeavour to make you join in worship with me that of which you*

2. Al-Qur'ān 2:132-4.

> *have no knowledge, obey them not; yet bear them company in this life with justice and consideration and follow the way of those who turn towards Me. In the end you all will return to Me. And thereupon I shall make you understand all that you were doing.*
>
> *O my son (said Luqmān) if there be (but) the weight of a mustard seed and it were (hidden) in a rock, or anywhere in the skies or in the earth, God will bring it forth. For God is unfathomable (in His Wisdom), All-Aware. O my son! Establish regular prayers, enjoin what is right and forbid what is wrong, and bear in patience whatever betide you; For this is firmness of (purpose) in the conduct of affairs.*
>
> *And turn not your cheek away from people in (false) pride, and walk not haughtily on the earth: for, behold, God does not love anyone who is arrogant, boastful.*
>
> *And be moderate in your pace and lower your voice for the harshest of sounds without doubt is the braying of an ass.*[3]

Short, succinct, perceptive and inspiring message of the Prophet Muḥammad ﷺ on the occasion of the farewell pilgrimage constitutes his *waṣiyyah* to the *Ummah*:

> *O people, listen to my words, for I do not know whether we shall ever meet again and perform Ḥajj together after this year.*

---

3. Al-Qur'ān 31:12-19.

O people! Allah created you from one male and one female and made you into tribes and nations, so as to be known to one another. Verily in the sight of Allah, the most honoured amongst you is the one who is most God fearing. There is no superiority for an Arab over a non-Arab and for a non-Arab over an Arab, nor for the white over the black nor for the black over the white, except on the basis of God-consciousness.

All mankind is the progeny of Adam, and Adam was fashioned out of clay. Behold! Every claim of privilege, whether that of blood or property, is under my heel, except that of the custody of the Ka'bah and supplying of water to the pilgrims.

O people of Quraish, don't appear (on the Day of Judgement) with the burden of this world around your necks, whereas other people may appear with the rewards of the Hereafter. In that case I shall avail you naught against Allah.

Behold! All practices of the days of ignorance are now under my feet. The blood revenges of the days of ignorance are remitted.

O people, verily your blood, your property and your honour are sacred and inviolable until you appear before your Lord, as the sacred inviolability of this day of yours, this month of yours and this very town (of yours). Verily, you will soon meet your Lord and you will be held answerable for your actions.

O people, verily you have got certain rights over your women and your women have certain rights over you.

Beware, no one committing a crime is responsible for it but himself. Neither the child is responsible for the crime of his father, nor the father is responsible for the crime of his child.

Nothing of his brother is lawful for a Muslim except what he himself gives willingly. So do not wrong yourselves.

All debts must be repaid, all borrowed property must be returned, gifts should be reciprocated and a surety must make good the loss to the assured.

O people, every Muslim is the brother of the other Muslim, and all the Muslims form one brotherhood. And your slaves! See that you feed them with such food as you eat yourselves, and clothe them with the same clothes that you, yourselves wear.

Take heed not to go astray after me, and strike one another's necks. He who (amongst you) has any trust with him, he must return it to its owner.

I am leaving with you what if you hold fast to, you will never go astray. The Book of God and the Sunnah *of His Prophet.*

O Lord, have I conveyed Your message?

These are the Qur'ānic instructions, and Prophetic traditions about *waṣiyyah*: First, to leave instructions about the way one wants one's wealth to be distributed after one's death – two-thirds according to the Islamic law of inheritance and up to one-third in accord with the will of the person. Secondly, to remind one's near and dear ones and all whom one's words reach, to be loyal to Allah and pursue the way He has illumined for humanity, to commend each other to fulfil honestly and sincerely all obligations towards Allah and towards the people, to make constant effort to purify one's soul and dedicate all that one has, knowledge, wealth, power and other resources for the promotion of good and justice in the world so as to seek salvation in the life to come. Khurram Murad's Last Will is a gem of such a *naṣīḥah*, not only meant for his wife and children, but for all Muslims and human beings.

Khurram was my dearest and closest brother and colleague. Our relationship spreads over a span of half a century. He represented a rare blend of scholarship and activism, vision and realism, commitment and compassion, love and integrity. The vow he made with his Lord in early youth, he strived hard to live by all his life through thick and thin, amidst seas of opportunity and tempests of adversity. He will be remembered as one of the architects of contemporary Islamic resurgence in the second half of the twentieth century. His writings will continue to guide the seekers after truth for a long time to come. His first book, "*Taḥrīk-e-Islāmī mein Kārkunon kē Bāhamī Ta'alluqāt*" (Mutual relationships amongst the workers of an Islamic Movement) written when he was a student and as part of a training package for the workers of the Islāmī Jamī'at-e-Ṭalabah Pakistan, and his Last Will, which is in your hands, represent two chapters of his life tied together by one theme and message. Khurram's main concern has always been how to be a true servant of the Lord (be one of the *Rabbānīyūn*). His life was dedicated to this search and effort; his writings are a recipe for that destination. The forty gems that go to make this wake-up call for all of us are his last gift to the workers of the Islamic movement in particular, and the *Ummah* in general. They provide a window to his heart and soul; they spell out clear-cut guidelines for self purification and preparation for the struggle of life. This work is a great *ṣadaqah jāriyyah* and will, for years to come, be a beacon of light in a world haunted by darkness and gloom. May Allah give the best of rewards to our young budding scholar Syed Abu Ahmad Akif for rendering this *waṣiyyah* into eloquent English prose. Akif's father and my dear brother and colleague Abul Khair Kashfi and Khurram's and my dear brother and life-long literary partner Zafar Ishaq Ansari, both have played a key role in the preparation and publication of this inspiring testament. May Allah bless Khurram's soul in eternal peace and bliss and may Allah reward young Akif, the translator, brothers Kashfi and Zafar Ishaq, and all my colleagues in the Islamic Foundation whose help made this publication possible.

Leicester
20th October, 2000
22nd Rajab, 1421 H

Khurshid Ahmad

Introduction

The Prophet, blessings and peace be on him, said: "No two nights should pass upon a Muslim who, while there are matters that deserve a will and testament, has not committed his will to writing."[1] I write this will as a direct fulfilment of the Holy Prophet's command.

None can escape death. It may come at any time, anywhere, suddenly. It can arrive at a time when no one is close by, or where those who are present are not the next of kin; or even in circumstances when such near and dear ones are present, one may be unable to say anything to them, let alone communicate one's last will about any matter. "Surely the term of Allah, when it comes, is not postponed. Did you but know!" (*Nūḥ* 71:4). "So they will not be able to make a bequest nor will they return to their homes" (*Yā Sīn* 36:50).

1. Bukhārī, "*Kitāb al-Waṣāyā*", and Muslim, "*Kitāb al-Waṣiyyah*".

When death arrives, one's links with all that exists in this temporal milieu are totally severed, one's control over everything ends, all material and mental resources are left behind, and one ceases to have the ability to do anything. The command to have one's last will and testament ready at all times has been given so that one may resolve all matters in the best possible of manners, to make due arrangements to meet all of one's obligations, to pay off one's debts in full, to absolve oneself of one's trusts, and to accomplish, as far as possible, all that one might have liked to.

Having one's last will ready at all times is also a reminder of life's frailty – the proverbial uncertainty of its measure – whether or not it shall remain beyond the day that passes. Such remembrance leads to that state and frame of mind which the Prophet, blessings and peace be upon him, has inculcated by saying: "If there is evening, be not certain of the morning's coming; and if there is morning, expect not that the evening too will surely arrive. Live in this world like a traveller or a wayfarer".[2]

Unfortunately, while being aware of all this, a lack of self-application and the usual procrastination were such that mornings came only to turn to evenings without my being able to write my will. It is only today, when 63 stages of life have passed, that I have finally come to write my last will and testament. Death, which was never far away, continues to come ever closer, and is now very near. In my case the delay

2. Bukhārī, "*Kitāb al-Riqāq*".

in writing the will is all the more lamentable and regretful as my case is quite different from that of ordinary Muslims who have been commanded to keep their last wills ready.

Since my first and very severe heart attack in November 1966, Allah has granted me 30 bonus years of life. In this long period I have faced the threat of impending death much more constantly and in an ever-increasing risk pattern than other ordinary persons. During these years I have suffered four more heart attacks, have been thrice removed by ambulance to intensive care (from which return is often uncertain), have suffered from angina pain for twenty years, have undergone four angiographies and have had two by-pass surgical procedures performed on me. And it's not just bypasses, but I have also had open-heart surgery because of a defective heart valve (which now consists of a plastic version). After the 1991 heart attack the angina pain has been constantly increasing.

Now a point has been reached when the third by-pass is being seriously considered. I have just arrived in England after spending two weeks in a Lahore CCU (Coronary Care Unit). Angiography is again planned for 8th February [1996] so that the future course of medical action can be considered. In all probability it will be another surgery unless Allah wills otherwise. I often joke that if something were to happen to me and my medical history were to be published, then the people concerned will not be surprised about why I passed away but will only wonder as to how and why I survived as long as I did.

Yet, in spite of all this, I could not write my last will and testament. But this negligence is not limited to the case of writing my will. Indeed, in all areas of life, I have done things that I shouldn't have done, and have failed to do much that I should have done, and this happened in spite of my knowing everything. A great part of my life was wasted in this neglect.[3]

It's not that I have been totally heedless of death's proximity in this long period of neglect or that I have never thought about writing my will. No, death has been close to my thoughts for a long time, and more so since 1982. Occasionally during the past five years I have also meditated on whether or not the next life-giving breath will arrive, and if it did come, whether the heart that had throbbed at Allah's command the last time will do so again. In order to strengthen my thoughts, precisely because of the consciousness of death, I have been praying – lest forgetfulness seizes me – while going to bed:

إِنْ أَمْسَكْتَ نَفْسِى فَارْحَمْهَا

O Allah, if Thou seizest my soul,
then be merciful to it.[4]

---

3. These lines represent the self-reproach of a deeply religious person with a highly sensitive conscience. They need not be taken literally.

4. Bukhārī, *"Kitāb al-Daʿawāt"*. The last words in the text that we have been able to locate in Bukhārī should be as: "O Allah, if Thou seizest my soul, then forgive it". Tr.

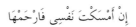

After the 1982 operation I wrote letters to all of you, and others too, as well as my will, and handed these to the nurse. These papers should be somewhere and upon finding them I will attach them herewith. For the past year I have been constantly thinking of writing my will once again. But my other writing tasks took so much of my time that I have not been able to come around to it. Indeed, I had started writing the will in the Lahore hospital, but then the process was discontinued. Now I am starting anew today, the 27th of January 1996 in Farooq's home. The work of the *Tarjumān [al-Qur'ān]*[5] is still on my head. I pray to Allah that He may enable me to complete the task in hand – the writing of my will.

This will is primarily addressed to Lam'at[6], (Ahmad, Hasan, Farooq, Farah, Owais, Faizah)[7], (Huma, Naushaba, Seema, Bilal, Maryam)[8], and all their children. If through them the general part of the will is publicly circulated, there is no bar from my side. But it is not my will that this be necessarily done.

---

5. A well-known monthly of the Subcontinent devoted to an elucidation of the teachings of Islam which Sayyid Abul A'la Mawdūdī edited for several decades and which Khurram Murad edited from 1991 until his death in 1996.

6. Mr. Murad's wife.

7. Mr. Murad's children.

8. The four ladies mentioned here are Mr. Murad's daughters-in-law, while Bilal is his son-in-law.

I

Death and *Ṣabr*

I am fully aware of the grief and sadness that all of you will experience upon my departure. The greater the love, the deeper the relationship, the more is the parting pain. I do not have the least doubt about the great attachment which all of you have for me. And so, keep the following few suggestions before you, and act upon them. Allah ﷻ will make this a means of perpetual benefit and benediction both for you and me. If you follow these suggestions that will also help you in taking control of your emotional state.

1. The anguish of hearts is a gift that reflects the compassion which Allah ﷻ has placed within you. The tenderness of the heart and the tears that roll from your eyes are also a manifestation of Allah's compassion [which He has endowed you with]. Consider the twinge of your hearts and your moistened eyes as Allah's bounty. The hearts that remain unmoved by the suffering around us and the eyes that fail to well with tears are a sign of one's being removed from

Allah's favour, of being impoverished. Remember well that this tenderness of emotions will act not just as the healing balm but will also be your support and a means of reward in the Hereafter.

2. It was on one such moment in life when, faced with a personal sorrow, the Prophet, blessings and peace be on him, said: "Indeed, while I am sad at this separation and my eyes are full of tears, yet I am fully satisfied with what Allah ﷻ has decided".[9] In these words of solace from the Prophet, blessings and peace be on him, you will come to find comfort and the resolve to persevere, and will also come to know the limit where you must stop in the expression of grief and anguish. Do bear in mind that even in sorrow you must have the intent to emulate the Prophet, blessings and peace be on him. This will bestow proximity with the Prophet and provide you support. What's more, you will also be rewarded for enduring this grief and affliction, and you will also be blessed with Allah's love for having followed in the footsteps of the Prophet: "... Follow me and Allah will

---

9. See Bukhārī, "*Kitāb al-Janā'iz*", *Bāb Qawl al-Nabī innā bika la Maḥzūnūn*. The translation of the text in this version would be the following: "While the eyes are flowing with tears and the heart is sad, but we shall say nothing except what will please our Lord. At your separation, O Ibrāhīm, we are indeed grief-stricken".

love you" (*Āl 'Imrān* 3:31). And part of these rich gifts, if Allah wills, will also keep reaching me.

3. Remember also the things which Allah ﷻ is not pleased with, those that provoke His Wrath. Do avoid them. Also avoid the mistake people make on such occasions[10] for they are inconsistent with true faith. Your hearts and eyes are not in your power. Nor is it required to exercise total control over your hearts and eyes. Rather, the compassion which your eyes and hearts give vent to is a gift from Allah Himself. But keeping the tongue in check is important and lies within your power. Do not say anything which is against the spirit *of riḍā bi'l-qaḍā'* (total acceptance of what Allah has decreed). Do not resort to lamentation and bemoaning, nor give vent to complaint and grievance, nor be seized with feelings of hopelessness and despair. The attitude of patience on your part would be a gift of immense value from you; a gift that would be extremely beneficial to me in facing the test that I shall encounter immediately upon the closing of my eyes. *In shā' Allāh,* for you too, such patience will be a cause of immense Divine reward and would be much preferable to uttering commonplace words and phrases that are meaningless and yield no result.

---

10. That is, when they suffer the bereavement of anyone who is very dear to them. Tr.

4. Most important of all, take care so as not to utter even a word of regret, nor let your heart be overwhelmed with that feeling. Certainly never think or say: "Oh, only if it had so happened or had not so happened ... then ...". The Prophet, blessings and peace be on him, has said that the word "*lau*" ("only If...") "opens the door to the act of Satan".[11] Allah has characterized it as a statement of those who disbelieve: "Do not be like the disbelievers who say to their brothers (who meet some mishap) in the course of their journey or fighting: 'Had they remained with us, they would not have died nor been slain; Allah makes such thoughts the cause of deep regrets in their hearts'". (*Āl 'Imrān* 3:156).

5. Such a manner of thought and expression is merely a cause of the pain that accompanies vain longings. For that which had to take place has taken place and in no way can it be reversed now. Also, because all that which was destined to happen did happen precisely in the manner, at the time, and at the place that it happened. Whatever 'preventive' measures might have been taken, there would have been no escaping the outcome. Remember these two things well and you will have at least achieved a measure of *riḍā' bi'l-qaḍā'*.

11. Ibn Mājah, "*Kitāb al-Zuhd*".

Remember, and remember again, and also remind yourself and everyone else, that Allah alone commands, He alone directs things in a given direction, and He alone disposes matters. The causes that appear before our eyes are only a means for the realisation of His Will. Only those who lack true knowledge about Allah have their vision enraptured by the means of this physical world, and the exaggerated notions that they entertain about the relationship between causes and effects becomes a barrier between them and their Lord.

For it is obvious that all that happens does so because of Allah's command: "No affliction ever comes but with Allah's permission" (*al-Taghābun* 64:11). Holding fast to this alone is the right mechanism to keep the heart on an even keel: "And whosoever believes in Allah, Allah provides guidance to his heart" (*al-Taghābun* 64:11). The misfortune which has struck could not have been avoided, and that which has not come about was destined not to happen. All men and jinn combined cannot forestall a harm nor cause any benefit. "The pens [to write the destiny] have been withdrawn and the scrolls have dried up",[12] said the Prophet, blessings and peace be upon him.

No one can live one second more nor die one second before the span designated for him by Allah. Whatever may be the cause, when the appointed time of death arrives none can delay it. Wherever and whichever manner of dying has been destined for a

12. Tirmidhī, "*Kitāb Ṣifat al-Qiyāmah*".

person, he will inevitably be drawn to his ultimate end. "Had you stayed in your homes, those of you destined to be slain would have gone to the places where they would be slain" (*Āl 'Imrān* 3:154). When all is written from before, why should there be a feeling of hopelessness or grievance or regret? All this has been made amply clear so that "you may not grieve over what escaped you" (*al-Ḥadīd* 57:23).

The following prayer of the Prophet, blessings and peace be upon him, is meant to be recited at the Station of Ibrāhīm. It is also an effective means of reaching lofty heights of cheerful submission and contentment with whatever Allah wills, the attributes for which Ibrāhīm is known. If you have not been reciting this prayer, begin doing so now, and with regularity; you will find it of great benefit:

اللَّهُمَّ إِنِّي أَسْأَلُكَ إِيمَانًا يُبَاشِرُ قَلْبِي وَيَقِينًا صَادِقًا حَتَّى
أَعْلَمَ أَنَّهُ لَنْ يُصِيبَنِي إِلاَّ مَا كَتَبْتَ لِي وَرِضًا بِمَا قَسَمْتَ لِي

O Allah, I implore Thee to grant me *īmān* (faith) that will saturate my heart; and true conviction to such an extent that I may know for sure that I shall receive only what Thou hast written for me; and satisfaction with what Thou hast apportioned for me.[13]

That which took place was what He had written. Remember also that all which He has taken was His,

13. *Kanz al-'Ummāl*, vol.2, *ḥadīth* no. 3657.

to begin with, for it is He Who had given it to us. And all which He had given us was meant to be for a limited period, provision [only] for an appointed time" (*al-Baqarah* 2:36), and thus it had to pass away. "All that is there [i.e. on the earth] shall perish" (*al-Raḥmān* 55:26). When such is the case, why should there be feelings of despair and grievous regrets? And what for should there be lamentation and bemoaning? So you better say:

لِلّٰهِ مَا أَخَذَ وَلِلّٰهِ مَا أَعْطَى

It was Allah's what He took away; and
it was Allah's what He gave,[14]

and further recite:

إِنَّا لِلّٰهِ وَإِنَّا إِلَيْهِ رَاجِعُونَ

Lo! We are Allah's and indeed unto Him we
shall return (*al-Baqarah* 2:156).

Such an attitude should not only be displayed upon my departure but whenever you are deprived of anything else in the world, howsoever dear it might have been. Whenever faced with a loss or inability to achieve something, keep your hearts, your thoughts, and your tongues in check with the help of these guidelines: you will be rewarded with an immense treasure of peace and comfort. All the cares of the

14. Bukhārī, "*Kitāb al-Janā'iz*".

world will vanish. You will also find great reward, for this is the very heart of *ṣabr* (patience): "Truly those who remain patient will be paid their reward beyond all measure" (*al-Zumar* 39:10).

6. I am exhorting you in such emphatic terms to be fully satisfied with whatever Allah wills for me and to abstain from being seized with despair and excessive grief because of two reasons: First, as is likely by the logic of cause and effect, the greater possibility seems to be that my death will be the outcome of my heart ailment. All the same, it is my belief that if, in spite of my very protracted heart disease, Allah has written some other cause of my death then that shall be the cause of it. Both are possible: I may be granted some respite, or death may come suddenly. Possibly I may pass away during some work or engagement, or immediately after that. In such cases, most people associate the immediate acts preceding death as being its cause. It is often said: "If he had done this or not done that then...". The thoughts of only a few go as far as to the Lord of all Causes. Few say: *Māshā' Allāh lā quwwata illā bi'llāh:* (As Allah wills; there is no Power nor Force other than that of Allah) (*al-Kahf* 18:39).

   I counsel you to remove your thoughts completely from causal relationships, be it a long illness or a hectic schedule of engagements, and focus your vision on the One Real Actor Who is hidden behind the curtain of the Unseen, and yet very much visible to those who use the vision of their soul and their insight. The cause could have been anything; it could have been an accident too. But that which happened had to happen, and had to happen at that particular time, and in that very manner. Whatever was done was done by Allah.

مَا شَاءَ اللّٰهُ كَانَ وَمَا لَمْ يَشَأْ لَمْ يَكُنْ

Whatever He willed, happened; and whatever He did not will, did not happen.[15]

For a long time the above line has been among the prayers which I have recited every morning. You should also do so after every *farḍ* Prayer. And also recite the following prayer with the intent of following the *sunnah* of the Prophet, blessings and peace be upon him:

لاَ إِلَـٰهَ إِلاَّ اللّٰهُ وَحْدَهُ لاَ شَرِيكَ لَهُ، لَهُ الْمُلْكُ،
وَلَهُ الْحَمْدُ، وَهُوَ عَلَى كُلِّ شَيْءٍ قَدِيرٌ

There is no god but Allah, the Unique One, Who has no associate to Him. To Him belongs all dominion and to Him belongs all grateful praise; and He has power over everything.[16]

15. Abū Dā'ūd, "*Kitāb al-Ādāb*".
16. Bukhārī, "*Kitāb al-Qadar*".

اللَّهُمَّ لاَ مَانِعَ لِمَا أَعْطَيْتَ وَلاَ مُعْطِيَ لِمَا مَنَعْتَ

O Allah, no one can prevent anyone from whatever Thou hast granted and no one can grant him whatever Thou hast prevented.[17]

This is all the more necessary specially in this materialistic age, when all things are interpreted simply in terms of material causation; keep your hearts and your eyes focused on: *Māshā' Allāh wa lā quwwata illā bi'llāh:* (What Allah wills [comes to pass]; there is no Power or Force other than Allah's) (*al-Kahf* 18:39). This is the best means to avoid the subtle form of *shirk* (associating others with Allah in His Divinity). This is also the best prescription for *ṣabr* (endurance in tribulation) *Wa mā ṣabruka illā bi'llāh* ("And you can find the power to persevere only from Allah") (*al-Naḥl* 16:128).

The second and more important reason for my advice is that it is quite possible that the immediate cause of my death would be my engagement in some work which pertains to the cause of Allah: perhaps while giving a talk or writing an article, while meeting someone or sitting in a gathering that is either part of my routine activity or one of an extraordinary nature. If the apparent reason is involvement

17. Al-Ṭabarānī, *Kitāb al-Du'ā'*, Beirut: Dār al-Bashā'ir al-Islāmiyyah, 1987, vol.2, p.1108.

in some such service in the cause of Allah, then placing blame on that activity would constitute not only disregard of the One True Cause that there is, but may also incur His Wrath through a disgruntlement expressed by the tongue or ill-will of the heart.

Nowadays there is also a visible tendency to blame the Jamā'at-i Islāmī, or its activities or its workers for keeping me overly busy, causing strain on my health. Minimizing the work of the Jamā'at is always high on any list of suggestions proposed for improving my situation. The advice to take a rest always means taking a rest from the Jamā'at's work. No mention is made of the numerous other mental and physical activities undertaken by me. I am averse to any suggestion of such a linkage and am always concerned that Allah too may be displeased by the same, that is, associating work in His cause with ill health. I take this opportunity to impress upon you that you should desist from making any such statements. If others were to say anything similar, they should also be corrected. Of course, none of us has control over the thoughts and feelings that might inadvertently come to one's mind and heart.

If work in the cause of Allah were ever to become a cause of my separation from you, we should be thankful to Allah. It is my prayer that if I am not to be blessed with martyrdom then at the very least I should die in harness, working for the cause of Allah. Perhaps this death in the line of duty may also be treated as martyrdom of some degree. It must be of some significance that the Qur'ān mentions dying as a separate category from being slain: "Were you to die or be slain in the way of Allah, then surely Allah's forgiveness and mercy are better than all the goods they amass" (*Āl 'Imrān*: 3:157).

It is my belief that the extra span of 30 years that has so far been granted to me[18] have been one of the blessings that have come my way due to my involvement in the work of Allah. And this bonus span has come my way in spite of so many heart attacks and operations, a bonus that came with great ease, so much so that two of the heart surgeries were performed without me incurring any expenditure. And on top of it all, this extra span was granted in such fashion that I have kept working harder than normal people do, whatsoever may have been the merit of my work. Indeed, I often consider that my work in these 30 years has been far more strenuous and productive than in the preceding period. Almost all of my written work has been done after 1981, when the series

18. This is an allusion to the massive heart attack suffered by the author in 1966. Ed.

of angiographies and surgical operations began following the second heart attack at Leicester. I am certain that whatever further period of life is granted to me will be in order that I continue to work in the cause of Allah. It is far more preferable that the period of life granted to me be insufficient compared to the tasks in hand than that the period be long but be spent merely in safeguarding against ill health, in resting, or doing nothing worthwhile.

7. Beyond *ṣabr* there is yet another stage of submission to and satisfaction with the Will of Allah; and that is the core of *riḍā' bi'l-qaḍā'*. Try to focus your vision on that. Attempt to perceive the goodness which Allah has placed for you in any apparently adverse situation. For Allah is all goodness: "In His Hand lies all good. All dominion belongs to Him. All praise is due to Him". Every act, every decree, every decision is from Him. Maybe because of your limited vision and consciousness, you may be unable to instantly perceive this good.

   The first beneficial aspect of adversity is that through *ṣabr* (patience) you will be rewarded with Allah's proximity and company, and will also be granted the choicest bounties and pleasures both in this world and the Hereafter. Had you not tasted some adversity, how could you have attained all this? If you were to ponder deeply, the greatest bounty of this world is transient just as the most distressing misfortune is short-lived. Neither the pleasures nor the pains of this world are real. For, in the first place, we all must pass away. Moreover, the bounty from Allah that has not been gratefully acknowledged will indeed become a bane on the Day when, as the Qur'ān says: "You shall most certainly be called to account about Allah's bounty" (*al-Takāthur* 102:6). That bounty will then come to haunt you as an affliction. Similarly, the hardship which we patiently endure in Allah's way is a harvest whose fruits shall not cease. That's why the Prophet, blessings and peace be upon him, said: "How wonderful is the state of the Believer: whatever his situation, it is excellent. And this is for no one except the Believer. If he is in prosperity, he is thankful [to Allah] and that is good for him. If he is in adversity, he endures it patiently, and that is [also] good for him".[19] You too should strive to earn such unceasing rewards. Celebrate your good fortune and state of satisfaction which comes your way; do not grieve over the transient pleasures which elude you, over being subjected to hardships that will soon go away.

Every state of adversity serves to purify your inner self and to train you. If you can begin to

19. Muslim, "*Kitāb al-Zuhd wa al-Riqāq*".

see this adversity as coming from the One "Who is Most Merciful to the Believers" (*al-Baqarah* 2:128), then you'll realize that hardships too are His gift; they are a means to enable you to meet the True Friend, a way to enable you to approach and encounter Him, and hence they are occasions to offer thanks to Him.

8. *Riḍā' bi'l-qaḍā'* is not a matter of accepting the unavoidable out of sheer helplessness. It is rather a matter of voluntarily submitting oneself to the Will of Allah ﷻ, and even cherishing it as an act of faith. It is also a matter of expecting reward from Allah in lieu of cheerfully submitting to His Will, of looking forward to the immense pleasure ensuing from that reward.

   The grief occasioned by my death would be because of the feeling that our relationship has been severed; because the pleasure of being close to each other, the pleasure of sitting together, the pleasure of talking to each other, has all come to an end. It is evident, however, that there is no escaping this separation. It is bound to happen, if not today then tomorrow. But it is precisely these pleasures which Allah has promised those who practice patience and piety (*Yūsuf* 12:90). So bounteous and everlasting is this reward that you simply cannot even imagine what it is like. "No mortal knows the extent of the bliss that has been laid up in hiding for them as a reward for what they did" (*al-Sajdah* 32:17). Also remember that this state of affairs will endure: "Their Lord promises for them gardens of abiding bliss" (*al-Tawbah* 9:21); "... therein they shall abide" (*al-Baqarah* 2:25); and "... they shall abide in them for ever" (*al-Tawbah* 9:22).

The state which has ended today Allah has promised to revive it for you in the eternal "tomorrow". The pleasure of being united once again, especially with spouses and children; the immense pleasure of mutual company – all that has been firmly promised by Allah. They shall be, says the Qur'ān, "on couches face to face" (*al-Ḥijr* 15:47). They shall also be occupied that Day "with joy" (*Yā Sīn* 36:55). "They and their spouses shall be in bounteous shade, reclining on raised couches" (*Yā Sīn* 36:56).

This transient pleasure that has been withdrawn today is nothing in comparison to the eternal joy. So, keep striving to live up to the dictates of *īmān* and righteous conduct. If we do so, it is Allah's firm promise that we shall be judged leniently, and we shall all be reunited and shall live together in eternal bliss. "Those who believe and whose offspring follow them in faith – We shall deprive them of naught of their work" (*al-Ṭūr* 52:21). "Gardens of Perpetuity, which they will enter along with those from among their fathers and their spouses and their offspring who do good; and the angels will come to them from every gate" (*al-Ra'd* 13:23).

9. I have not inculcated in you to practice *ṣabr* (patience) in the commonly understood sense of the term, nor have I done so in the manner in which people attempt to persuade others to do so. Nor do I wish to do so now. All the same, by means of all what I have counselled you so far I have tried to lead you on to the path of *ṣabr,* making that path both wide and easy to follow. I have led you to the gateway *of ṣabr* and have handed over its keys to you. I hope that by using these keys you will be able to open for yourselves the portals *of ṣabr* and proceed along that path and ultimately open for yourselves the portals of *jannah* (paradise). The prescription for a successful outcome, for peace and satisfaction, not just at this time, but throughout your lives, lies hidden in *ṣabr*: "Thus your Lord's gracious promise was fulfilled to the Children of Israel, for they had endured with patience" (*al-A'rāf* 7:137).

As far as my feelings regarding death are concerned, I can only communicate to you what I feel today; what they will be tomorrow, only Allah knows best. If this attitude is in keeping with His liking, may He strengthen it; if not, may He reform it.

First, the fear of death is natural. I have never been totally without such fear, neither am I free of it today, nor perhaps will I be at the time of death – fear of the pangs of death when it comes; fear of the suffering which might follow death. No one, not even Prophets, can be altogether free of this natural fear. The Prophet Moses experienced a feeling of being pursued when he embarked on his secret departure from Egypt (*al-Qaṣaṣ* 28:21). Likewise, when he threw down his staff and it turned into a writhing serpent, then too he turned back out of the natural feeling of fear (*al-Qaṣaṣ* 28:31). As for the pangs of death, it is a suffering that one experiences here in this world. The narrations of 'Ā'ishah (may Allah be pleased with her) concerning the last moments of the Prophet, blessings and peace be upon him, which one reads in the book *Insāniyat Mawt ké Darwāzé Par* ("Mankind at the Portal of Death") by Abu'l Kalām Azād, makes one shiver at the thought of death.

Second, I must also confess that in spite of my having constantly prayed for being endowed with that state of inner desire whereby one looks forward to meeting Him[20] and to be granted the privilege to look at His Gracious Countenance, I have not yet succeeded in experiencing that state. Even at the mere thought of death [which is the doorway to meeting the Lord] fear overcomes the desire [to meet the Lord]. Even the promised exaltation at seeing His Face has

20. Al-Nasā'ī, "*Kitāb al-Sahw*".

not enabled me to overcome this fear. Or, perhaps, I am not aware of how this fear of death which is rooted in human nature can be combined with the state of desire and joy of meeting Him which is rooted in the intellect. If any support is to be found in this regard, it is to be found in the *ḥadīth* narrated by 'Ā'ishah (may Allah be pleased with her). The Prophet, blessings and peace be on him, said: "Allah cherishes to meet him who cherishes to meet Allah, and Allah does not like to meet him who does not wish to meet Allah".[21] On hearing this 'Ā'ishah raised the very natural question about her natural dislike for death: "But each of us dislikes death", she said. Clarifying this, the Prophet, blessings and peace be upon him, said: "I do not mean this. But when a Believer is promised rewards from Allah and His pleasure and paradise – then he looks forward to meeting Allah".[22]

In any case, when I view my own deeds then the hope of Divine reward fades and fear begins to dominate over the love and the desire of the heart to meet the Lord, and my heart cries out, in the words of the Prophet Moses: "My Lord, I stand in need of whatever good Thou mayest send to me" (*al-Qaṣaṣ* 28:24). Perhaps it's not so much the fear of death that restrains the desire to meet the Lord as the fear of being punished for my evil deeds.

Third, as far as this world is concerned, the state of my feelings at this moment is such that deprivation

21. Al-Nasā'ī, "*Kitāb al-Janā'iz*".

22. Bukhārī, "*Kitāb al-Riqāq*".

from no worldly good would vex my heart, although, of course, it is Allah Who knows best. No material loss hurts me any more. There is no desire or longing the unfulfilment of which causes me to be sad or woebegone. In fact, such is my state of mind that if some cash were to come my way, I am left wondering as to which desire of mine I should try to fulfil with it, except spending it on the needs of others or in the Way of Allah, or leaving it behind so that it might take care of someone's needs after my demise.

Yet, if I do find any association with anything, then it is with my writings and speeches which I could not make publication-worthy, or those thoughts and feelings in my heart and mind which have remained unexpressed in writing. I also think of those whose happiness largely depends upon me so as to say: how they shall fare after me; or those who apparently have no human guardian to look after them, especially Faizah [my daughter] who is presently deprived of joy; in future too the prospects for her well being are few. Under whose guardianship will she be? How will she be treated? Be that as it may, we can only gain comfort from complete trust in Allah.

Of course, many writers who have gone before me, have left behind unfinished ideas and unpublished manuscripts much worthier than mine. So if it is not Allah's will that all of my works be made ready for publication, why should I be concerned? What great success have I accomplished anyway from the work that has already been published? Or, for that matter, how much benefit has been derived from all the outstanding publications of others? And who knows what extra time Allah may have kept in store for me, just as so much productive time was made available to me since 1981. Perhaps this latest illness of mine too may become a means to provide me the time required to finish the many incomplete tasks. As far as we humans are concerned, the Only One who can really look after us is "the Ever-Living Allah Who shall never die" (*al-Furqān* 25:58), and He alone shall suffice for us, as the Qur'ān says: "Allah alone suffices as a Helper" (*al-Nisā'* 4:81).

Over the years, my desires and aspirations with regard to all of you have generally been expressed as prayers. I have hardly been able to look after your education and upbringing and am deeply aware of this shortcoming of mine. I hope that on the Day of Judgment none of you will hold me accountable for this lapse. All the same, it is beyond my power to thank Allah enough for the fact that He has made all of you far more good and righteous, and far more active workers in the cause of Faith than I could have wished for. People give me credit for this but I know that all this has been achieved by your own striving; and if anyone at all has contributed to your good upbringing, it is your mother. But, of course, this is solely Allah's gift for you and me.

These desires and wishes, some expressed, others hidden deep within, might have always been there, or perhaps, have always been there. When in 1971 we separated from each other in Dhaka, the hopes of being reunited were slim. This separation, which was to last for more than two years, was like the separation that is brought about by death. I left home on December 16, 1971 when bullets were flying all around. While even animals have a place of their own to dwell, for a few days I did not know where to seek refuge. It was not my wish to seek the help of any human being for shelter, and by the grace of Allah I did not have to do so. Then Allah not only gave me refuge, but gave me a dignified one. He provided me with protection in such manner that even my presence in the camp remained unknown to others. One day bullets flew over our heads as we lay still on the ground. Allah kept me safe and sound and then united me with all of you. Indeed, not just then, but the rest of my life ever since can best be described in the words of the Qur'ānic verse: "He sheltered you and strengthened you with His help and provided you of the good things" (*al-Anfāl* 8:26).

In camp life [as a prisoner of war in India] while I lived in a cage-like prison, it was possible for me to have the joy of privacy even while living in the midst of a crowd of 300 people, for no care or concern occupied my mind. As for you all, I had left all thoughts about you to Allah, just as I am doing today. I had entrusted you to the care of Allah without the least feeling of anguish or apprehension, even though quite obviously my attachment with you was most intense and you were always in my thoughts. During this time, when Allah provided me an almost daily opportunity to turn to Him with utmost devotion in the very late hours of the night before dawn, all my desires for you turned into words of supplication. From those days till today, whenever and to whatever extent Allah has enabled me to beseech Him, those prayers have been for you. I may not have been able to do much for you in practical terms, but at least I have kept asking Allah for every possible good for you. And now I am committing to writing and enjoining upon you in this testament all whatever I have been praying for. Do keep striving for whatever I have wished you to become. This is my last wish and will.

My heart bears witness that Allah has given you amply all that I had prayed for. And so it is my belief that in the future too Allah shall answer my prayers and bestow great rewards on you both in this world and in the Hereafter. I have mentioned "this world" before the Hereafter for two reasons: first, because it is the life of this world that provides the key to all of one's accomplishments in the religious realm and in the Hereafter; and second, because Allah Himself has mentioned "this world" before the Hereafter in the prayer He has taught us: "Our Lord, grant us what is good in this world and grant us what is good in the Hereafter" (*al-Baqarah* 2:201).

II

Message for Successful Living

⟨ 1 ⟩

As far as this temporal world is concerned, the first thing I have prayed to Allah for you is that He may grant you the richness of heart, that He may enable you to keep yourselves impervious to the world. Remember, the real wealth of this world and the Hereafter lies in the richness of heart. This is the fountainhead of all good. On the contrary, love of this world is the root of all evil. It is my feeling that Allah has granted all of you some degree of this richness. In other words, my prayers have been answered. This reinforces the belief that many other of my prayers must also have been answered, even those that relate to myself.

Value this wealth – the richness of heart – that you have gained. Protect it, strive to increase it, and attempt to fill in its gaps. Piety lies not in altogether shunning this material world, but in eschewing its love. Do enjoy the legitimate bounties of Allah in full, but do not be a slave of any of them. Never develop an attachment with them of a kind that cannot be broken. Eat well, dress well, live well. You may earn and keep wealth too, but never have your heart in such things. Their availability or absence should be of no consequence to you. Strive to achieve a state of mind in which you accept not just Allah's bounty but also when He tests you by subjecting you to meagreness of worldly resources. Whether it be a sumptuous meal or a piece of coarse bread, or even the prospect of starvation, each state should be considered as Allah's gift for you. Be happy and at peace in each state. When the heart is free of the cares of this world, why would you disobey Allah on Whom you are dependent for all your worldly needs? And then, why should you be sad on losing the riches of the world? Never incur Allah's Wrath for the sake of this world; never make yourself sick and weary on account of this world.

2

The second thing which I have prayed for you with regard to this world is that never may Allah make you dependent upon any of His creatures; may He make you dependent on Himself alone. May you never have to spread out your hand before anyone but Allah. The Prophet, blessings and peace be upon him, had sought a special oath from some of his selected Companions that they would not beseech anyone for anything. The result was that even if they were to drop their whip while riding, they would stoop to retrieve it themselves and not request anyone to pick it up for them.[23] Although I could not act fully on this principle, I have always kept it as my ideal. I desire this same ideal for you. As far as possible, try to act on this principle. The way to achieve this is to simply link all your expectations with Allah and disassociate all your expectations from whatever other human beings may possess or whatever may be in their power; and give up hopes regarding whatever might be in the hands of human beings!

وَاجْمَعْ الإِيَاسَ مِمَّا فِي يَدَيْ النَّاسِ

"Make me give up all hope regarding whatever lies in the hand of people

اللهُمَّ اقْذِفْ فِي قَلْبِي رَجَاءَك وَاقْطَعْ عَنِّي رَجَاءَ لِمَن سِوَاك

O Allah, instil in my heart all hopes with Thee and cut off all hopes with ought other than Thee".[24]

Most of the evils in human relationships and most of the sorrows that we encounter are the result of broken expectations. By severing your hopes from human beings, not only will these relationships be freed from being vitiated but you will also be able to rid yourselves of your grief and sorrow.

3

The third theme of my prayers has been to ask Allah to grant you an abundance of livelihood that is

23. Abū Dā'ūd, "*Kitāb al-Zakāh*".
24. Ibn Mājah, "*Kitāb al-Zuhd*".

ḥalāl and *ṭayyib* (lawful and pure); to grant you the means of income that should at least be enough for you to meet your needs with ease, so that while being contented with whatever you have, you may be happy and have a due portion of worldly enjoyments.

A minimum of worldly resources is necessary even for the protection of faith. Do not be negligent in trying to secure some portion of the world. Indeed, this is part of *'ibādah* (worship) and is essential in order to ensure a degree of excellence in the other acts of *'ibādah*. So do try to earn at least this minimum of livelihood, considering it a part of your religious obligations. At the same time, hold fast to the belief that you are bound to receive what Allah has ordained for you. Treading on forbidden paths will not earn you any more than what is your apportioned share. Also keep in view the directive of the Prophet, blessings and peace be upon him: "Be moderate in seeking [wealth]".[25]

4

Man is encumbered with a trust from Allah which includes a number of tasks pertaining to the world, to seeking livelihood and meeting one's obligations to others. Strive to fulfil all these tasks with absolute integrity, while never losing sight of the requirements of honesty. Fulfil all your obligations with a full sense of responsibility. Try to do your work in the best

25. *Kanz al-'Ummāl*, vol.4, *ḥadīth* nos. 9291 and 9306.

possible manner, seeking to conform to ever-higher standards of excellence. Aim at success even in your worldly efforts, and keep the standards as high as possible. Religious devotion does not consist of disregarding the world. All that you undertake will be reckoned as acts of devotion provided you perform them for the sake of Allah alone, and keep them free of sin and disobedience.

《 5 》

My real desire – in fact the only desire – is that you should live your lives as devoted servants of Allah, as His totally dedicated subjects. The essence of man's servitude to Allah lies in cheerfully carrying out whatever would please Him, and in adhering to His commands and prohibitions. In addition, it also requires that extra effort over and above fulfilling mandatory commands, that engaging in the labour of love which, while not obligatory, leads to His Pleasure. True love makes the lover fix his gaze on the face of the beloved with the result that he carries out all the behests of the beloved, in fact, even those indicated by the movements of the eyelids.

This state of devotion is well-expressed by the recitation of the following words three times after the Prayer:

رَضِيتُ بِاللَّهِ رَبًّا، وَبِالإِسْلَامِ دِينًا، وَبِمُحَمَّدٍ
صَلَّى اللَّهُ عَلَيْهِ وَسَلَّمَ نَبِيًّا

I am satisfied with Allah as my Lord,
with Islam as the true religion, and with
Muḥammad as the true Prophet (blessings
and peace be upon him).

He who has achieved this state of feeling has truly savoured the taste of *īmān*".[26]

Also accept with good cheer all the events that occur by Allah's will. In other words, act as He orders you to act, and do so with wholehearted happiness. Moreover, be happy regardless of the circumstance in which Allah places you. To be happy with whatever Allah has apportioned for a person is well expressed in the following words which are usually recited after the Prayer is over:

لاَ إِلَـــهَ إِلاَّ اللَّهُ وَحْدَهُ لاَ شَرِيكَ لَهُ، لَهُ الْمُلْكُ،
وَلَهُ الْحَمْدُ، وَهُوَ عَلَى كُلِّ شَيْءٍ قَدِيرٌ

There is no God but Allah, the Unique One, Who
has no associate to Him. To Him belongs all
dominion and to Him belongs all grateful praise;
and He has power over everything.[27]

اللَّهُمَّ لاَ مَانِعَ لِمَا أَعْطَيْتَ وَلاَ مُعْطِيَ لِمَا مَنَعْتَ

O Allah, no one can prevent anyone from whatever
Thou hast granted and no one can grant him
whatever Thou hast prevented.[28]

---

26. Bukhārī, "*Kitāb al-'Ilm*"; Muslim, "*Kitāb al-Īmān*".
27. Bukhārī, "*Kitāb al-Qadar*".
28. Al-Ṭabarānī, *Kitāb al-Du'ā'*, Beirut: Dār al-Bashā'ir al-Islāmiyyah, 1987, vol.2, p.1108.

《6》

Strive to become Allah's sincere devotees. On the one hand there should be no worldly act that is not done as an act of servitude to Allah, not even such acts as sleeping, eating, dressing, speaking and laughing. The Prophet, blessings and peace be upon him, engaged in all these acts. But he was God's devotee *par excellence.* As a consequence of that, every facet of his life, even the most ordinary of chores, was an act of devotion to Allah. It is important that every act of life should be for the sake of Allah, and for His Pleasure alone, as the Qur'ān says: "And of men is he who would give himself away to seek the pleasure of Allah..." (*al-Baqarah* 2:207).

Without such spirit, even the most religious of acts – prayers, reciting the Qur'ān, martyrdom, and *infāq* (spending in the way of Allah) – would all be merely worldly acts. Imbued with this spirit of total dedication, even the smallest religious act, and all acts of worldly life, would stand heavy in the scale of Divine Justice. If you are able to achieve this state of sincerity, even a little effort would suffice in imparting the colour of Allah in your life and soul. All the evils of the world – in men's souls, in their lives, in their mutual relationships – have their roots in lack of sincerity. Lack of sincerity in matters pertaining to religious activities specially leads to very evil effects.

Designate your *niyyah* (intent) purely for Allah and strive always to keep it so. This brief and simple prescription is the gist of true religious faith and of the desire to shape your life completely according to that mould. It is also the most effective formula to remember Allah at all times. This is the perpetual *dhikr* (remembrance), one that suffices for all occasions.

❮ 7 ❯

Doing everything for Allah's sake would be easy if you were to always bear in mind that each act of yours will be presented before Allah for His judgment. Any act would only be acceptable if it was for His Pleasure. Together with this, also keep your vision focused on *jannah* (paradise) and *jahannam* (hell-fire), on the reward and punishment that has been promised, on seeking the reward and avoiding the punishment. The longing for paradise and the fear of hell are the two elements that will strengthen your resolve to tread the path of obedience. It is for this reason that the Prophet, blessings and peace be upon him, came with a mission to serve both as a *bashīr* (bearer of good tidings) and a *nadhīr* (warner) so that he could prepare men for lives of submission to God by inspiring them with desire and fear.

❮ 8 ❯

Hold fast to the remembrance of Allah. Make every effort in this regard. Remember Allah at all times and in all states – standing, sitting, lying down. Bring forth a peaceful state for yourselves for, as the Qur'ān says, it is "in the remembrance of Allah that hearts find rest" (*al-Ra'd* 13:28).

❮ 9 ❯

Remember always that "He is always with you" (*al-Ḥadīd* 57:4). If there are two of you, then He is the third. He sees all, He hears all, and He knows even that which lies within the deepest folds of the heart. What will happen tomorrow, He alone knows: "Verily, Allah knows everything" (*al-Baqarah* 2:29).

❮ 10 ❯

Remember also that the universe is governed only by Allah's command, and no one else's. Everything is His, and is subject to His authority: "He has power over everything" (*al-Baqarah* 2:148). "His is the dominion over the heavens and the earth" (*al-Baqarah* 2:107). "When He decrees a thing, He need only say: 'Be', and it is" (*Yā Sīn* 36:82).

❮ 11 ❯

Always keep in mind that everything we enjoy is from Him and so to Him we owe all praise and all gratitude. "Whatever bounty you have is from Allah" (*al-Naḥl* 16:53). "All praise be to Allah, the Lord of the whole universe" (*al-Fātiḥah* 1:1). If you succeed in gaining the perception that all that we enjoy comes from Him and also learn to show gratitude to Him for His bounties then you shall have reached the essence of *īmān.* Such praise and gratefulness shall make the Scales tilt heavily in your favour on the Day of Judgment. Whenever you gain even the slightest of worldly rewards, be it a morsel or a drop, or when you are saved from some loss or have the opportunity to do any good, express your gratitude, by saying: "*Al-ḥamdu li'llah* "(All praise and thanks be to Allah)" (*al-Fātiḥah* 1:1). Be grateful for everything that you receive. You cannot imagine how joyous your lives will be when your mornings begin with the song of Allah's Praise and the notes of this song flow from the instruments of life throughout the day until it ends at night on the same note of thanksgiving it began with. You cannot imagine how dear your lives will be in the eyes of Allah: "If you were to give Him thanks, that is what He likes for you" (*al-Zumar*, 39:7). "Why should Allah chastise you if you are grateful and believe?" (*al-Nisā'* 4:147).

Praise Allah and pay gratitude to Him until He is truly pleased with you. His Pleasure is such an immense bounty that if He is indeed pleased with you, then it would be beyond your power to thank Him enough. The Prophet, blessings and peace be on him, said: "All grateful praise be for Thee till Thou art pleased; and all grateful praise be for Thee that Thou be pleased".

12

Remember well that you are destined to meet Him. The invitation for that may come at any time. Your whole life is nothing but a preparation for this

Meeting. "Let every soul consider that which it sends forth for tomorrow" (*al-Ḥashr* 59: 18). "And to Him you shall return" (*al-Baqarah* 2:245). "And to Him you shall be mustered" (*al-Mu'minūn* 23:79). "And unto Him is your destiny" (*al-Mā'idah* 5:18).

The more you keep that Meeting in mind, the greater would be the enthusiasm with which you shall prepare for it; and the greater is your preparation for meeting Allah, the better will be your chances for eternal salvation.

《 13 》

The non-formal ways and means of remembering Allah are innumerable: just repeating "Allah, Allah" in your heart; contemplating on His attributes; keeping in mind that He is always watching you. As often as possible and to whatever extent possible, always keep your vision focused on Him.

《 14 》

Try also to learn by heart the words of prayers, the designated supplications (*ad'iyah*) and the phrases of remembrance (*adhkār*) which have been taught by the Prophet, blessings and peace be upon him. Try to memorize them as much as possible, if not in the original Arabic, then in your own tongue. Make it a point to recite them regularly. Try to instil in yourselves a passion for raising your hands in prayer. Like all forms of expression, this too needs training and learning to develop a personal disposition and state of mind. Try to remember Allah as frequently as He grants you the succour to do so, especially in the last watches of the night. It would help if you were to establish a definite set of prayers. You are aware of my chosen set of prayers: it appears in my work *Qurb-i Ilāhī ké Āsān 'Amalī Ṭarīqé* ("Easy Ways to Attain Proximity to Allah") (Lahore, Manshūrāt).

❮ 15 ❯

The Qur'ān is all Allah's remembrance *(dhikr)*, light *(nūr)*, mercy *(raḥmah)*, guidance *(hidāyah)* and panacea (*shifā'*) for the inner ailments (*Yūnus* 10:59), those that lie hidden within the breasts of people. Do develop as much passion for reading and studying the Qur'ān as you can. Try to spend as much time in the company of the Qur'ān as possible. If circumstances do not permit opening the pages of the Book, try to recite a bit from the portion which you have engraved on your hearts. The Holy Book has it all: Allah's praise, the exaltation and glorification of Allah, the affirmation of His absolute unity as the Lord, and statement entrusting oneself and one's affairs to Him, the supplications to Allah ﷻ, of Allah's Beautiful Names, the reminders of our ultimate Meeting with the Lord, the remembrance of Allah ﷻ both with the tongue and by the heart and the other organs of the body.

❮ 16 ❯

The most comprehensive ensemble of all forms of remembrance is *ṣalāh* (Prayer). Never be neglectful of *ṣalāh*. Try to instil every *ṣalāh* with as much of *khushū'* (submissiveness, humility and reverence) and true remembrance of Allah as possible. The very purpose of Prayer is, as the Qur'ān says, to remember Allah: "Establish Prayer for My remembrance" (*Ṭā Hā* 20:14). The effort to attain *khushū'* is not difficult at all. Concentrate on anything: on yourselves with the feeling that Allah is watching you; or concentrate on Allah, or on His attributes, or on the Ka'bah, or on the words that you are reciting, or on the thought that this may be your very last Prayer.

❮ 17 ❯

Make full effort to observe congregational Prayers. Offering *ṣalāh* in congregation is 27 times more rewarding than the one offered alone. He who offers the *Ishā'* Prayer in congregation is like him who has performed Prayer for half a night. Similarly, he who offers the *Fajr* Prayer in congregation is also like him who has prayed for half a night. According to many commentators of the Qur'ān, the words describing the Believers as those "who sleep but little at night-time" (*al-Dhāriyāt* 51:17), apply to those who sleep after praying *'Ishā'* in congregation. For sinners like us, Allah has made attaining the reward so easy.

How unfortunate would it be if we are unable to reap its rewards even after this facility.

《 18 》

Continue seeking help from Allah through *ṣabr* (patience) and *ṣalāh* (Prayer). If He wills then every act of yours will be facilitated; you shall succeed in every effort. I have already impressed upon you about *ṣabr.* The best way of attaining it is to remember Allah and observe *ṣalāh*. Wherever Allah urges people to observe *ṣabr* [in the Qur'ān], there also occurs mention of remembering, glorifying and praising Allah and offering *ṣalāh*. Keep these two – *ṣabr* and *ṣalāh* – close together, and contentment and peace will pervade everything about you: your heart, your mind, your work, and your life as a whole.

《 19 》

It is highly desirable that we be obedient to Allah in all matters pertaining to our relations with our fellow beings. In these relations and in your conduct and dealings follow the course that will please Allah. This should be your foremost consideration. It should be the goal that you should concentrate on achieving.

Spending in the way of Allah ["And they spend of what We have provided them" (*al-Baqarah* 2:3)] has a very deep-rooted relationship with *ṣalāh*. Wherever Allah has urged the establishment of *ṣalāh*,

He has also urged *infāq* (spending in the way of Allah) and payment of *zakāt* (obligatory almsgiving). Wherever there is mention of prayer and devotion and penitently seeking God's forgiveness in the late watches of the night or early dawn there is also reference to generously spending wealth for the sake of Allah. The virtues of forgiveness and forbearance have also been linked with helping the poor and feeding the destitute. [Here are a few instances]: "Then as for him who gives (for the sake of Allah) and acts with God-fearing and confirms that which is good..." (*al-Layl* 92:5-6). "...and those who spend (for the sake of Allah), and who ask pardon (from Allah) in the hours of the morning" (*Āl 'Imrān* 3:16). "Those who spend in ease as well as in adversity and those who restrain their anger and pardon others" (*Āl 'Imrān* 3:133). "They forsake their beds, calling upon their Lord in fear and in hope, and spend out of what We have given them" (*al-Sajdah* 32:16). "They sleep but little at night-time. And in the morning they ask for (Allah's) forgiveness. And in their wealth there is rightful claim of those who ask (others for help) and for those who are deprived" (*al-Dhāriyāt* 51:17-19).

Engrave these verses on your hearts, keep them before your eyes and always act according to their spirit; bring your transactions, your attitudes and your character within their fold. They shall suffice for you. But most of all pay special heed to the important implications of spending in the way of Allah.

❮ 20 ❯

Do not hurt any creature, specially a human being, and most importantly, a Muslim, by any word or action of yours. Just as doing every act for the sake of Allah is the very essence of true faith, avoidance of causing hurt to anyone is the gist of Allah's commands. Whichever principle of the *Sharī'ah* you might ponder over, you will find this factor common in some form or the other: the *ḥudūd* punishments, the rules regarding divorce, the principles of commercial transactions and social intercourse. This is a very pervasive principle, so much so that it extends even to very minute matters. Hence people have been told not to conceal anyone else's objects even by way of a practical joke, or even point a weapon at anyone, nor to occupy the seat of someone who has gone away for a short while, nor to jump over other people's heads to find a place in the front rows of a congregation; nor to peep into other people's homes, nor pry into the affairs of others, nor read someone else's mail, nor get up at night in a way that would disturb others. Indeed, the principle is of such wide-ranging application that it is simply not possible to enumerate all such instances. Simply stated, make this principle your guiding light and the scale of all moral judgment: that you shall not cause any injury to anyone by your words or deeds. In dealing with others this should be your guiding principle.

Very often we are not cautious enough in the words we utter. Restrain yourself from speaking or acting in any manner hurtful to others. Of course, the exception will be when others might be hurt in the course of our doing something in order to fulfil a requirement of the *Sharī'ah* and there is no way to avoid such a course of action. Even then do seek pardon from Allah.

⟨ 21 ⟩

The principle to accord a humane treatment to people and avoid hurting them is not restricted to Muslims. It is only that such behaviour has been specially stressed in regard to Muslims. All of Allah's creatures are "His family",[29] so much so that animals too are included within this fold. To keep a camel hungry or weigh it down with an unbearable load, not to give it enough rest, or to slaughter an animal within sight of another, or to use a blunt knife for slaughtering an animal or to steal a bird's young from its nest, or to put an anthill to fire are all forbidden acts. When such are the guidelines for the treatment of animals, you can well imagine what are the rights of human beings, whether they be sinful Muslims or non-Muslims.

⟨ 22 ⟩

Any act by which someone is hurt, or his person, possession or dignity are subjected to any loss is

---

29. *Kanz al-'Ummāl*, vol.6, p.171.

absolutely forbidden; it is forbidden in the same way as is pork, alcohol or usury.

It is significant that the command [in the Qur'ān] forbidding eating and drinking during obligatory fasting is immediately followed by the command forbidding usurpation of other people's possessions by false means (*al-Baqarah* 2:187-188). Together with the prohibition of the four items of food,[30] the deliberate concealment of Allah's commandments has been equated with filling one's stomach with hell-fire (*al-Baqarah* 2:173-174).

And remember, violation of Allah's commandments is worse than their concealment. Indeed, while some leniency may be shown when unlawful food is consumed in extreme cases of emergency, no such mitigation on account of extraordinary situations is possible in case of violating such prohibitions as not to usurp others' property, nor backbite nor defame nor slander. The punishment for these is only hell-fire. Even worse would be the fact that Allah would not talk to such offenders, nor cleanse them of their sins. (See *Āl 'Imrān* 3:77.)

There is no pardon from Allah in cases where personal rights have been violated; forgiveness may only come from the person aggrieved – either directly or when Allah makes it possible for that person to grant such pardon. Just save yourself from such acts; I

30. That is, carrion, blood, flesh of swine, and that over which any name other than Allah's has been pronounced. (See *al-Baqarah* 2:173. Tr.)

repeat, save yourselves. And if you were to violate others' rights, obtain their forgiveness here in this world or else you'll be left absolutely destitute and bankrupt on the Day of Judgment.

23

Most of all, protect your tongue. I have found just one way of preventing oneself from falling headlong into hell: just keep your mouth shut about others except when you speak well of them. Never speak ill of others in their absence, nor level any accusation in their presence that you cannot prove. Never speak ill of others. Moreover, if you find people engaged in backbiting and you can neither get away from the scene, nor prevent others from backbiting, immediately begin to recite *istighfār* (supplication seeking pardon from Allah). Never try to find a justification for your wrong actions. These others whose rights you may violate include your spouse, parents, children, in-laws, brothers and sisters, servants, those who live in your neighbourhood, fellow-workers and those who are your transient neighbours such as fellow-travellers. Having a relationship with others does not entitle you to violate their rights. On the contrary, because of this relationship, the action of violating their rights becomes even more grave. Just keep your mouth shut with regard to others unless you have something good to say. I find no other way of salvation but this.

《 24 》

Move beyond the concern of merely not violating the rights of others; concern yourselves with how you can fulfil your obligations towards them. To start with, avoid hurting others, but don't stop at that. Be benevolent to them, serve them, fulfil their needs. You cannot even imagine the rewards brought forth by good deeds that are apparently insignificant: helping someone board a vehicle, removing an obstacle from the road, helping in a chore like drawing water from the well, lending someone an item of daily use, looking at someone with a smile, treating someone with respect, striving to help a Muslim – all these acts are superior even to such meritorious acts as *i'tikāf* (confining oneself within a mosque for total religious devotion during the last ten days of *Ramaḍān*) in the Prophet's Mosque. As long as you are busy helping someone in the fulfilment of his needs or serving a fellow human being Allah will also keep meeting your needs and helping you. For your acts that alleviate the sufferings of others in this world, Allah shall remove your suffering on the Day of Judgment. If you cover someone else's shortcomings, Allah will cover your failings on the Last Day. If you feed a hungry man or tend to the sick, you shall encounter Allah there, right beside him.

《 25 》

I specially enjoin you to protect yourselves from the evils that have become commonplace. Never find fault with others; instead, keep your own shortcomings in mind. Inquisitiveness is forbidden; never become involved in it. If you come to know of someone's sins, try to cover them. Let alone narrating them behind his back, do not embarrass him by mentioning them even in his presence. You will not gain anything from this; it will only injure someone's heart. Never accuse anyone without proof. Slander and false accusation are also forbidden. Nor combine slander and false accusation with backbiting.

《 26 》

In order to cultivate your character on the lines of these injunctions, you will have to purify your heart of a number of evils – evils that lie at the root of every wickedness and corruption. The first of these is vanity – thinking highly of oneself while considering others lowly and insignificant. Be modest; adopt humility. You cannot say anything about yourself with certainty until Allah exonerates you on the Last Day and accepts your good deeds. If He were to reject you, who shall be more contemptible than yourself? What could be more foolish than to consider yourself superior to fellow criminals in the prison that this world is! Until the Lord of the Day of Judgment pronounces His verdict, consider every Muslim better than yourself. Keep your gaze on the virtues of others, not on their shortcomings. Only mention their good points, not the bad ones. At the same time, do not go about openly announcing your own faults or disparaging your own self. Be humble and modest in your manner of living and conduct before Allah as if you are an abject and degraded slave. Do not raise your voice like an ass. Do not display arrogance. What a folly it is to be haughty over your body which is destined to turn into pus and become a meal of insects and germs!

27

Free yourself from miserliness and meanness of the heart. The more humble and polite you are, the more strongly will you believe that everything belongs to Allah and that whatever you give now shall be returned in the form of a much greater reward. The more you believe that if you were to stop charity it would come to haunt you, the easier will it be for you to be magnanimous. The more your heart is filled with the Greatness of Allah, the more generous your heart will become. The greater your ability to negate ego, status, arrogance, vanity, wealth, and the more you feel that you have not discharged your responsibilities to the full – the more happy will you become. Give away your wealth today, give it away readily, sacrifice your self-esteem, cleanse yourself of the love of this world and Allah will expand your heart. He shall make you so benevolent that you will have made yourself deserving of the paradise whose expanse will embrace the heavens and the earth.

❮ 28 ❯

The softness and compassion of the heart, the warmth of love, the benevolence and tranquillity of the inner self, all constitute an immense wealth. If your heart is at peace, your attitude too will be serene, the words will be gentle and the tone kindly, and there will be an all-encompassing tenderness in your interaction with others. "Adopt tenderness".[31] "Whoever is deprived of tenderness is deprived of all good".[32]

Love conquers the world. That which can be had with tenderness and leniency cannot be won by harshness. Whatever can be won with love will not come by enmity or hate. When your loving and hating and your giving and your withholding is for the sake of none except Allah, your *īmān* will become perfect.[33] The Prophet, blessings and peace be upon him, was and is a mercy for the whole world, one full of love and compassion for the believers. By talking in a harsh tone, by being mean in your transactions, by putting on a grim face, you shall not gain anything.

31. Muslim, "*Kitāb al-Birr wa al-Ṣilah wa al-Ādāb*". There is an obvious error in the text in Urdu in which the *ḥadīth* reads "*Iyyākum wa 'l-rifq*" whereas it should read: "'*Alaykum bi'l-rifq*". This is a clear case of a slip of the pen. Tr.

32. *Ibid.*

33. See Abū Dā'ūd, "*Kitāb al-Sunnah*".

By softness and love and compassion, your heart shall be rewarded with inner peace and a feeling of sweetness, your worldly affairs shall become smooth and pleasant, and all this will ensure Allah's Paradise in the Hereafter.

29

Do not hate the sinners, only their sins. Do not aid Satan in his task by damning and anathematizing the sinners. Instead, help them fight Satan by praying that they be guided to the Straight Path and obtain their deliverance. Be watchful of your own sins, keep reciting the Qur'ānic verse: "Do you not love that Allah should forgive you?" (*al-Nūr* 24:22) and try to understand the meaning of the Qur'ānic verse: "And man has been created weak" (*al-Nisā'* 4:28). Realize that everyone's life is full of both good and evil and that every group is composed of both the good and the bad. This realisation will make it easier for you to deal with the sinners around you in the manner that Allah and His Prophet, blessings and peace be upon him, have desired.

When it comes to shortcomings and sins, give others a greater allowance than you would give yourselves. Consider others more worthy of being pardoned than you regard your own claim to be forgiven. Be less harsh to others than you are on your own self. Be less demanding of others than you are of yourself. If Allah wills, you shall find much good in such conduct.

❮ 30 ❯

Remember to fulfil the rights of your close relatives and observe the best of behaviour with them; remain in touch with them; always keep them in your mind and designate a share for them in your wealth: this is an immensely good deed which Allah greatly likes. Very early in the Qur'ān, Allah states that one of the traits of those who have gone astray is that "they sever what Allah has commanded to be joined" (*al-Baqarah* 2:27). Be kind and benevolent to your next of kin; spend your wealth on them. The same goes for your neighbours, specially the neighbours who are also related to you. (See *al-Nisā'* 4:36). Among the destitutes and the orphans, your next of kin have a prior claim upon your benevolence. That has been repeatedly emphasised in the Qur'ān: "... the orphan who is next of kin" (*al-Balad* 90:15).

I am indeed surprised as to how those people who recite the Qur'ān and desire to practice its teachings are so neglectful of this great act of goodness. Do apportion not only a part of your wealth for them but also take out their share in terms of time, attention and love. When Allah gives you wealth, do not forget to earmark a share for them. According to a *ḥadīth* in Bukhārī and Muslim: "Your benevolent behaviour towards the next of kin will serve to increase your wealth and life-span". Such acts of goodness shall also earn you Allah's mercy on the Day of Judgment. According to a *ḥadīth*, when Allah had completed all creation, the womb sought His refuge from all those who strive to tear such Divine links apart. Allah therefore had it proclaimed through His Prophet: "He who unites you [by linking blood relationships], shall be united with My Mercy; he who severs you, shall be dissociated from My Mercy".[34]

Keep before you the principle of "first consideration for those that are closest, then to those that are next to them"; but do not forget anyone – parents, your family members, siblings, uncles and aunts, and so on and so forth. Remember each according to his importance, also the friends of your parents, those dear to them, your guests, and your neighbours. Specially be mindful of the Prophet's saying that: "The greatest good is to be good to the friends and dear ones of your father".[35]

31

Tolerate disagreements. Do not let difference of opinion with others or their criticism of you affect your relationships. Accept criticism with humility, tolerance, open-heartedness and high spirit. Always accept the right thing and disregard whatever is wrong.

Never be overcome by cowardice in accepting responsibility for your mistakes, nor shy away from accepting your faults. Do not be excessive when criticizing others nor display miserliness when praising them.

---

34. Bukhārī and Muslim.

35. Muslim, "*Kitāb al-Birr wa al-Ṣilah*".

Anyone who abuses you to your face is actually degrading himself. Why should you be angry? What do you lose if someone backbites and gossips against you? If you choose to remain silent, the angels will answer on your behalf. Otherwise you shall be caught in a web of anger and revenge, defending your self-esteem in the face of abuse, thereby committing ten times more sins. Through maintaining silence, you will not only receive the angels' support but also have credited to your account the good deeds of your abusers. Far from burning yourself in the fire of anger and revenge, you should, in keeping with the custom of Imām Abū Ḥanīfah, send gifts to your denigrators [for, in the ultimate, their abuses will be conducive to your own good].[36]

Never fall into the trap of countering your critics, specially in public. Consider carefully and coolly the objections raised by them. If they are right, correct yourself; if they [say or] write something false, forgive them. You do not lose anything by forgiveness; neither would your prestige be lessened, nor would there be any heightening of ill-will and bitterness. On the other hand, you would perhaps taste the sweetness that flows from winning hearts. There is nothing more useless than getting entangled with others in a series of criticism and counter-criticism. By staying away

---

36. This is an allusion to a *ḥadīth* to the effect that on the day of Judgment God will take away the good deeds of a person and put it in the account of him whom he had either beaten, or defamed, or abused, etc. See Muslim, *"Kitāb al-Birr wa al-Ṣilah wa al-Ādāb"*. Tr.

from this wasteful activity, you will save time, time which can then be devoted to acts of goodness and which will earn you God's reward.

If you were to follow these principles everywhere – in the family, at home, among friends, in the neighbourhood, at work, or in your social and religious life – you shall find peace and satisfaction. If not, then you'll be stricken with constant anguish and suffering. Nothing is more pleasant than forgiving the injuries caused by your opponents. And when you start doing everything for Allah's sake, then you will realize how easy all this can be.

32

Throughout this temporal life, always keep your vision fixed on the task of inviting people to the true faith, and on the effort to make it prevail. Until your very last keep this as your goal and mission. Never allow any other purpose to supersede this supreme objective nor let any other concern prevail over this passion, specially the concern to acquire worldly benefits.

There can be no greater act of perpetual charity[37] than the fact that a person starts to do a good deed because of your inspiration. And if that person were not just to engage himself in the good deed but also

37. In Islam distinction is made between those charitable acts that end with that act (e.g. feeding someone who is hungry) and those that will continue in perpetuity (e.g. establishing a school, a hospital, making an endowment for a good purpose or planting a tree that provides shade to the wayfarer). Tr.

make others engage in it, then the perpetual reward for charity shall have increased manifold. If this work is one of *da'wah*, of the struggle to establish the true faith and make the word of Allah prevail, or to ensure enforcing the penalties prescribed by Allah to curb evils, or the revival of some *sunnah* of the Prophet, blessings and peace be upon him, then your reward shall be in line with what the Qur'ān calls *aḍ'āfan muḍā'afah* (doubled and redoubled) (*Āl 'Imrān* 3:130). Not only that, you will also witness the fulfilment of the tiding: "With Us there is more" (*Qāf* 50:35). Consider not any act of goodness too small, nor one of evil too trivial, yet try to understand the rankings of human actions and act accordingly. No extent of *nawāfil* (supererogatory acts of worship) can equal the smallest measure of a *farḍ* (obligatory prayer or any other obligatory act). Fulfil all obligations, but the crowning obligation is to strive in the cause of Allah. Do not fall into Satan's trap by engaging in acts of lesser good while ignoring acts of greater good.

Do not even come close to falling a victim to the illusion that would occupy you with means to such an extent that you lose sight of the end: "We are doing this so as to be able to work better towards our real goal." Never has that hoped-for occasion on which the vision was to be re-aligned come back to present itself. Nor allow yourself to be caught in the fallacy that states: "We should reform ourselves, then we will do that" or "First let us gain full knowledge of faith, and then we will remove the discrepancy between what we preach and what we practice at a later date". Bear well in mind that that time will never come. Nor be enticed by the self-delusion: "Not today, tomorrow surely". "Just let me get over this, and later on ...". The stage for that shall never come.

Save yourself from the spreading cancer of despair. In today's atmosphere of hopelessness this is the most common disease. Adopt the best strategies for the advancement of Allah's cause. Allah has a right over your intellect. If your cause suffers a defeat or setback, if people do not listen to you, if they do not support you, it would be your religious duty to find out the causes of all that and to try to remedy the situation.

The desire to see people come into the fold of Islam in the greatest of numbers, and in the very least of time, the desire to witness that our efforts are crowned with success quickly, and that the true faith comes to prevail are all quite legitimate. However, as an individual, you should have only one objective in this world: to earn the right to Paradise by thoroughly achieving your potential and fully satisfying the requirements of the struggle. Apart from this, you should not seek anything else.

While continuing to struggle in the way of Allah, keep your heart alive and burning with the desire to attain martyrdom. Until the time that Allah enables you to lay down your life in His cause and gain the glory of martyrdom (*shahādah*), continue to extend your *shahādah* by way of your wealth, good deeds, *da'wah,* through your speeches and writings and in every other manner. Be not neglectful in this sphere of fulfilling your duty nor lose your share in these acts of sacrifice.

⟪ 33 ⟫

In order to struggle in the way of Allah, it is essential to have an organized group life. This is important not only to achieve your own reformation and training but also in order that you remain resolute in the way of Allah. Never dissociate yourself from the group nor from the principles and etiquettes which hold it together. By so doing, not only will the group be strengthened, but you yourselves will benefit a lot from your association with it. You will be able to hold on to your commitment with your cause, and contribute to keeping the people together and will yourself be able to remain associated with the group. You will be able to observe the discipline of organized life while remaining conscious of its rightful ways and limits. You will be able to follow the principle of mutual consultation, punctuality, fulfilment of your obligations, and giving good counsel stemming from goodwill for them. These are only some out of the many benefits that will accrue from being a part of organized group life.

At times group existence passes through the phases when it is seized with the feeling of despair. Do not allow your sense of disappointment to lead to a severance of your links with the group. If Allah grants me the time and the ability to write, I shall leave behind my autobiography or a diary. From this you will be able to see how, in spite of my disagreement and disappointment [with the *Jamā'at*] following the events of 1970, and which progressively increased, I resolutely maintained my fidelity to the cause to which I had committed my allegiance and resolutely fulfilled my obligations arising from that fidelity. On the other hand, you will observe that some persons parted company [with the *Jamā'at*] on their very first exposure to the fire of disagreement and disappointment.

34

When you strive to make Islam operative in your own life, or in the lives of others, or in the society, never be neglectful of the immense wealth that is wisdom. In this connection, I specially urge you to go through my talk on the topic of "*Ḥikmat-i Dīn*" ("Wisdom in *Dīn*") and my editorials of *Tarjumān al-Qur'ān*'s issues of October through December 1992. Conforming to the principles of gradualness and refraining from extremism are very important parts of this wisdom. Avoid excessive debate and discussion of small and peripheral issues. At no cost should you engage in unnecessary confrontation with the common people or provoke their wrath. Try to look at their variant opinions, even their mistakes, in a favourable context. Do not withdraw yourself from them unless you are required to support something that involves disobeying Allah. Extreme caution should be taken when using the words *ḥalāl* (permissible) or *ḥarām* (forbidden); in fact, try to avoid them to the maximum possible extent. Such was the way of our early forebears.

﴾ 35 ﴿

Your own home is in your control. Strive to enforce the commandments of Allah within its precincts. Establish Allah's rules in your home. Your most important task should be to arrange and maintain your home according to the Will of Allah. After your own self, the things about which you shall be asked and required to explain on the Day of Judgment will be those that are within your power. Most important amongst these is your home. The reformation of your home is dependent upon your own reformation and vice versa. When your home operates according to the Will of Allah, you shall be rewarded with the immense wealth of peace and satisfaction. Although no home is secure against external influences today, yet your efforts can make a great difference.

Make the Qur'ānic verse: "Guard yourselves and your kindred from the Fire..." (*al-Taḥrīm* 66:6) the guiding light for your family life. Let the spirit of this verse be central to the daily routines of your domestic life and for your mutual relations. Whether it is the material possessions of your home or the food and drink, or the education and training of your children, or their entertainment and future welfare, or the relationships between spouses and the treatment of the children, or the conduct towards your employees, always make sure that no action of yours leads you to the hell-fire. The more you keep your vision focused on this principle and the more you strive towards this end, the more your domestic life will be heavenly and is likely to lead you to the attainment of Paradise.

This is not to say that this constant concern with hell-fire will deprive you of all worldly pleasures and enjoyment. No, not at all. Given such a concern, your home life will be permeated with mutual caring; there will also be much love and mutual affection; and there will also be happiness that emanates from mutual forgiving and tolerance. There will also be a lot of scope for enjoyment from things that are clean and lawful, and of course, the home will have all permissible adornments. All these will be there since they are to save oneself from Allah's Wrath.

No two human beings are alike. When they have to live together, it is natural that there will be some discord and dissent. In this regard, husbands must remember what kind of husband was the Prophet, blessings and peace be upon him, in his home. They should remember his instructions to men with regard to their wives. Women have the right that their husbands be caring and affectionate to them. When the Prophet, blessings and peace be upon him, went on a journey he made it a point to take one of the wives along. He also made an effort to spend some time with them every day. He joined them in their pleasantries, took them out for recreation, and even joined them in races.[38] The Prophet, blessings and peace be upon him, said: "The most perfect believers are the best in conduct among you and the best among you is he who is best to his wife".[39]

When some husbands disciplined their wives, the latter visited the wives of the Prophet, blessings and peace be upon him, to lodge their complaints. Upon this the Prophet, blessings and peace be upon him, said: "Women often come to my wives with complaints against their husbands. These people are not the better ones amongst you". He further said: "Be kind and gentle towards women. A believing man should not dislike a believing woman [that is, his wife. Ed.]. If he does not like one of her habits, then there will certainly be other habits that he will like" (The same will apply to women in respect of men.)

Our disinclination to come to terms with realities when we encounter disappointments, our disinclination to be flexible with others – that is the root cause of the vitiation of human relationships. Avoid that. Be mindful of your children's self-respect, but do not slacken in their upbringing. Be mindful of your own conduct: no one perceives inner contradictions of a

38. Bukhārī, "*Kitāb al-Manāqib*".

39. Tirmidhī, "*Kitāb al-Īmān*".

person's behaviour more sharply than his own children. And so, whatever you may do or not do in your home, always avoid contradictions between what you preach and what you practice.

Teach your children good manners. I am fully aware of the areas in which there have been problems in this regard and where they continue to go unchecked. Therefore I am hurt. Such good manners include the manners to be observed in greeting and meeting others, during conversation, in showing respect to elders, in entertaining guests, and at the dining table.

It was my desire that my grand children complete the Qur'ān before doing anything else. I desired that their relationship with the Book be well established and the love of the Qur'ān be embedded in their hearts. It was also my wish that they do not go to English medium schools so that at this tender age their chaste memories are not engraved with rhymes like "Ba Ba black sheep", but are adorned instead with the verses of the Qur'ān, with the sayings of the Prophet, blessings and peace be upon him, with poems in praise of the Prophet, with the poetry of our great poets like Ḥālī and Iqbāl, and the masterpieces of our religious literature. Unfortunately this could not be.

Now, at the very least, do endeavour to impart them whatever you can by way of Qur'ānic education and religious instruction. This should be done in such a manner that the respect and love of these subjects are ingrained in their hearts. If this is done my soul will be immensely pleased.

I do not pass any edict against television being unlawful. But for Allah's sake, keep your homes free of this curse and filth, and also from books and photographs that are lewd. Try to make the atmosphere of your home as pure and clean as is possible for you.

If regular religious gatherings can be organized so much the better, but even within your busy daily routines try to maintain the remembrance of Allah, and urge others to do good and abstain from evil. Also narrate to them the stories *of jihād* (holy struggle) and *shahādah* (martyrdom).

﴾ 36 ﴿

You will require both strength and resolve to practice the things I have counselled in this will. The fountainhead of this strength and resolve is the belief in, constant fear of, and continual engagement in, preparing ourselves for our inevitable return to Allah, our destined encounter with Him, and the conviction that the true success is the success of the Hereafter; that our true life is the life of the Next World. You have to just decide on this once and for all. The earlier you do this the better. Then everything you do will be for this very end – the Hereafter; every moment that you live, every penny that you spend, and every relationship that you have, will all be in a manner that would conduce to your well-being in the Next Life: "Let every soul consider what it has sent forth for the morrow", says the Qur'ān (*al-Ḥashr* 59:18).

Many people try to ride two boats at the same time and suffer in both ways. You should decide that you have to earn the Hereafter and only the Hereafter from the whole of this temporal life. And even when you seek to earn the world, that should also be in order that you might earn the Hereafter. If you do so, you will join the ranks of those "who realise that they have to meet their Lord and that to Him they are destined to return" (*al-Baqarah* 2:46). You shall have attained that *khushū'* (submissiveness and humility) which is something so valuable that if you are devoid of it, no amount of knowledge will be of any avail. On the other hand, if you have *khushū'* it will be easy for you to observe *ṣabr* (patience) and *ṣalāh* (Prayer). Both of these are the keys to all the good of this world and the Hereafter.

The secret of attaining *taqwā* – the token of a successful life – also depends upon your clearly deciding and resolutely persevering with the decision that your goal is the Hereafter. The underlying objective of all worldly concerns and preoccupations should be to earn the Hereafter. If you always keep the Hereafter in view, you shall not only attain *taqwā* but the blessings of this world and the Next shall also be yours. All kinds of blessings shall be showered upon you from every direction, you shall be free of every consternation, you shall be granted livelihood from the sources that are not even in the far reaches of your imagination. You shall also become the rightful inheritors of Paradise. In order to achieve this, keep the thought of death and the different stages through which one will have to pass in the Hereafter close to your heart.

37

Even if you have the determination to achieve success in the Hereafter, make it your main objective and then strive to achieve this objective in the manner that it deserves. You will still be able to attain it only when you have fully achieved the blessing of "belief in the Unseen". Whether it is Allah or the Hereafter, both belong to the realm of the Unseen. These are the realities that are beyond the power and reach of the senses; they are hidden from your sight and vision. Belief in the Unseen will help you in your determination to achieve success in the Hereafter; it will add strength and endurance to your resolve. Neither heaven nor hell are within the realm of sensory perception and still you must seek and yearn for one and have dread and abhorrence for the other. You have not seen the All-Compassionate Lord, but still do believe in Him and cultivate an awe for Him in your heart.

❮ 38 ❯

In order to taste the sweetness of *īmān,* strive to infuse the love of Allah and His Prophet in your heart. Once this love is there, *īmān* shall penetrate into every sinew of your body; it will make its place in the depths of your heart. Allah has said: "But those who truly believe, they love Allah more than all else" (*al-Baqarah* 2:165). And Allah's Prophet, blessings and peace be upon him, has said: "You cannot be a true believer until I am dearer to you than everything else in the world".[40]

There should be no difficulty in understanding this love. Each one of you knows what love is. You know how restless one is to get close to whomsoever one loves; what pleasure one feels even in taking the name of the beloved and in taking that name again and again; the earnest zest with which one strives to win over one's beloved, and the extent to which one dreads the displeasure of the beloved. Just keep examining to what extent you have attained this love. Peep into your heart and see what is the place of Allah therein. The same shall be your place before Him.

The prescription for attaining this love is easy: commit yourself to follow in the footsteps of the Prophet, blessings and peace be upon him; try to live your life as he lived it; colour yourself in his colours; hold dear all those purposes that were dear to him;

40. Tirmidhī, "*Kitāb al-Daʿwāt*".

walk on the paths that he loved to walk upon: "Say, if you indeed love Allah, then follow me..." (*Āl ʿImrān* 3:31). Also keep praying for all this.

اللَّهُمَّ إِنِّي أَسْأَلُكَ حُبَّكَ وَحُبَّ مَنْ يُحِبُّكَ وَحُبَّ عَمَلٍ
يُقَرِّبُنِي إِلَى حُبِّكَ

O Allah, I ask of Thee Thy love, and the love of
him who loves Thee, and the love of the deed
that will bring me close to Thy love.

اللَّهُمَّ اجْعَلْنِي أُحِبُّكَ بِقَلْبِي كُلَّهُ وَأُرْضِيكَ بِجَهْدِي كُلَّهُ

O Allah, make me love Thee with my heart, the
whole of it; and make me devote my effort, the
whole of it, to please Thee.

اللَّهُمَّ اجْعَلْ حُبَّ قَلْبِي لَكَ كُلَّه وَسَعْيِي كُلَّهُ فِي مَرْضَاتِكَ

O Allah, make the love of my heart, the whole
of it, be devoted to Thee, and my striving, the
whole of it, be directed to whatever
pleases Thee.

Call to mind very frequently Allah's bounties, His favours, and do mention them as much as you can. Call to mind and mention all kinds of bounties, those that were and are for all of us collectively, as well as those that were and are for you in particular; the material bounties as well as those that pertain to the realm of intellect and spirit; both the big and the small.

⟪ 39 ⟫

Remember well, no matter how hard you try it would not be possible to abstain totally from sin: "All of you are sinners; all of you are guilty".[41] If you would not have sinned, Allah would have created another genre of beings to whom He would have granted free will; they would have sinned and then sought His pardon, and then He would have pardoned them. So do not lose heart because of your sins. Do not be caught in the noose of hopelessness or give up your resolve [to do the will of Allah]. Seek Allah's pardon and keep treading the path of your Creator. His Hand of Kindness is always open. He Himself calls you towards Himself: "He calls you that He may forgive you" (*Ibrāhīm* 14:10). He calls you in the morning so that the sinners of the night may come forth; He extends His Hand in the evening that those who have trespassed during the day may come and seek His forgiveness and He may forgive them.

Be quick in seeking forgiveness. Spread out your hands towards Allah to seek His forgiveness as soon as you have sinned. The stains on your heart shall have been wiped away and it will shine bright. The darkness shall recede and there will be light. The faith that shall have gone away from you shall return. Do not ever delay this.

---

41. Tirmidhī, "*Ṣifat al-Qiyāmah*".

Recite *istighfār* frequently. The Prophet, blessings and peace be upon him, recited it more than 100 times every day.[42] Do not let the frequent repetition of your sins keep you away from seeking pardon. Sinning repeatedly and then seeking forgiveness just as frequently does not come within the definition of a state of deliberate insistence upon sin. It is sinning with impunity and then not attempting to seek forgiveness, and attempting to explain your sins away that comes within that meaning of insistence on sinning.

Shed your tears after every sin. Do not shy away from this. Self-impose a burden of atonement whenever you sin, such as giving away something as *ṣadaqah* (alms); forgiving someone for any wrong he may have done you, or a certain number of *raka'āt* of Prayer. Hasten in repenting and seeking forgiveness. Do not relent in this. The door for seeking forgiveness is open at all times but the best time of all is the early hours of dawn before *Fajr*. Even if Allah enables you to devote just a few moments, do so. Place your forehead on the prayer mat and seek forgiveness with flowing tears. I strongly urge that you do so.

If you have sinned with regard to the rights of others, then together with repentance and seeking forgiveness, it is also essential to ask for the pardon of those concerned and to make up for the damages.

---

42. Al-Ṭabarānī, "*Kitāb al-Du'ā'*" *ḥadīth* nos. 1809-1835.

Recitation of *istighfār* will open the door to that forgiveness which is essential for entry into heaven: "And hasten to forgiveness from Your Lord and to a Paradise as vast as the heavens and the earth..." (*Āl 'Imrān* 3:133). Not only that, this will lead to other blessings as well – material prosperity, relief from difficulties, and a feeling of ease even in adversity.

40

The last thing that I will say is that whatever of Allah's blessings you receive – His forgiveness, His rewards, His pleasure, and eternal comfort – all will be by dint of your own effort. You will receive these because of your actions. This will be the reward of your own striving: "No mortal knows what bliss has been kept in store for them as reward for what they did" (*al-Sajdah* 32:17), "... man will have only what he strives for" (*al-Najm* 53:39); "that his striving will soon be seen and then he will be rewarded for it with the fullest reward" (*al-Najm* 53:40-41). Life is the most precious thing of all. Assume full responsibility for it. Just as a shopkeeper tends his store, a businessman takes care of his trade, or a farmer carefully looks after his farm, you too should take the reins of your life in your hands. So, do open and close the shop at the right times, settle the accounts on a daily basis, and tend to your farm. When you strive to set yourself and your life right, when the desire to succeed here and in the Hereafter overwhelms you, Allah will keep on opening new avenues of growth and progress for you. This is His promise: "And those who strive hard in Our cause, We shall certainly guide them to Our ways (*al-'Ankabūt* 29:69).

Allah only wants two things from you: one, determination, and second, effort and struggle, both accompanied with the purity of *īmān*. After that you will find nothing lacking in His patronage and reward: "But he who desires the Hereafter and strives for it as he should, and is a true believer, those are ones whose striving shall come to full fruition" (*Banī Isrā'īl* 17:19).

Always be wary of your actions. Adopt *khushū'* (submissiveness and humility) towards Allah, He Who is Merciful and Compassionate. Have faith in His Grace and Mercy and in the truthfulness of His promises. Associate all your hopes with Allah. Call upon Him with fear and good expectation. Keep reciting: "And He is merciful to those that believe" (*al-Aḥzāb* 33:43).

III

Journey to Fear and Hope

When I reflect about my ultimate fate, the state is one between hope and fear. It is, however, fear that is dominant. It is within the power of Allah that at the time my end comes, hope might dominate over fear. I am full of regrets, full of sorrow, and full of shame over my misdeeds. When I read in the Qur'ān about those who will be in the forefront of the exalted ones (*al-sābiqūn*) in Paradise, or those who will enjoy Allah's proximity in the Hereafter (*al-muqarrabūn*), a twinge of sorrow sparks off in me. It was not all that difficult. And then I remember what the Qur'ān tells us: "And not far thence, Paradise shall be brought close to the God-fearing" (*Qāf* 50:31).

Yet I lost all the opportunities. For no good reason I emburdened myself with sins, with sins which have caused nothing but destruction. It is difficult not to give up the yearning to be part of those who will be in the forefront of the good ones, or those who will enjoy the proximity of Allah in Paradise. But this seems like too good a dream to come true. Then I think of *aṣḥāb al-yamīn* (the people of the right hand), those whose good deeds will be heavier and who will be saved, even though they would have committed sins. When I look at the pans of the balance, here too there does not seem much hope for I do not think I have made myself deserving of being included in this category, even though this would have been easy.

Then I read the description of *aṣḥāb al-shimāl* (the people of the left hand), the people of Hell. I can hardly believe that I would be included among them. What will happen, then? My state seems to be the one described by the verse: "There are those who have confessed their sins; their good works had been intermixed with evil, and perchance Allah will turn to them in mercy. Allah is All-Pardoning; All-Compassionate" (*al-Tawbah* 9:102). I have my share of good deeds and of sins too and the two are intermixed. I also confess my sins, those that I know of and those too of which I am unaware. A Day will come when people will confess their sins (*al-Tawbah* 9:102); and will confess them with pangs of regret and say: "If only we had listened and understood" (*al-Mulk* 67:10).

So here I stand, in the words of the Prophet, blessings and peace be upon him, "confessing and owning my sins to Thee", and I do so before the coming of that Awesome Day. The tears of repentance are also flowing in accompaniment with a feeling of regret. This gives rise to some hope: it is well within the power of Him Who is All-Pardoning and All-Compassionate to look upon me with His Mercy, to compassionately turn to me and clasp me with His Grace. Maybe out of Mercy He would not hand out my Record of life publicly, and that which has hitherto remained hidden from others will remain hidden; maybe He would decide to show deference to the favourable opinions in which others have held me in this world so that the good opinions of so many believers are not proved untrue. He might cover me entirely with His Forgiveness and Mercy. Even he who was the closest to Allah[43] has said that there was no hope for him unless Allah were to encompass him in His Mercy. I recite this three times: "Thy Forgiveness in much vaster than my sins and Thy Mercy is much greater a source of my hope than my deeds", and my ears strain to hear from somewhere the heartening proclamation: "Rise, your sins are forgiven".

How many a time when I went to Madinah my eyes have been flooded with tears in expectation of Allah's forgiveness. And how many a time, while reciting my reverential greetings to the Prophet, blessings and peace be upon him, I have, in my imagination, rubbed my eyes against his feet, the feet of my master. At such times my heart has been stirred by the hope of the fulfilment of the following promise: "If, whenever they wronged themselves,

43. That is, the Prophet, blessings and peace be on him. Tr.

they had come to thee and had prayed to Allah for forgiveness, and had the Messenger [also] prayed for their forgiveness, they would have found Allah All-Forgiving, All-Compassionate" (*al-Nisā'* 4:64).

Repentance and yearning, and yearning and repentance: this is the total harvest of life.

Were you to act upon all the good things I have brought together here, or have said or written in the past, that will be a very precious gift for me in the stages that lie ahead of me. That will indeed be the greatest service that you will render to me, your highest act of fidelity and your greatest favour to me.

To close, I enjoin upon you to fear Allah in the manner Allah Himself has said: "Believers! Fear Allah as He should be feared, and see that you do not die save in the state of submission to Allah" (*Āl 'Imrān* 3:102). And with this, I entrust your religious devotion and the end of your deeds to the care of Allah.